Entertaining Friends

Easy Does It with 101 Rules of Thumb

Peggy Healy and Marcelline Thomson

ISBN-10: 1501096702

Healy, Peggy and Thomson, Marcelline
Entertaining Friends· Easy Does It with 101 Rules of Thumb

First U.S. Edition 2014
Designed by Vicky Forsyth-Smith
Drawings by Vicky Forsyth-Smith; Cartoons by Ted Dawson

CONTENTS

"My doctor told me to stop having intimate dinners for four. Unless there are three other people."

- Oscar Wilde

Dear Reader,

We're here to sing the praises of the dinner party, intimate or not. Brunch, lunch, cocktail and dessert parties too.

Why? Because nothing in the world makes us happier than being with our friends. Getting together over food is one of life's great pleasures, one we suspect our ancient ancestors enjoyed when gnawing on a bone in a cave. Today, texting, emailing, Instagramming and tweeting just don't cut it. They are poor substitutes for the bonding that entertaining creates, especially when we do it at home.

This little handbook is a lighthearted and practical guide to how to make it easy. For fun we give you the old rules of entertaining etiquette, side by side with new ones for today's lifestyles. Knowing a few rules simplifies things. We also give descriptions of memorable parties, tips and inspirations, cartoons and quotes. Plus some short cuts and a dozen failsafe recipes, from canapés to salads to main courses to desserts.

We hope you enjoy this romp through the rules.

Peggy and Marcelline
November 2014

CHAPTER ONE

Entertaining Style, Themes and Numbers:
Getting Started

Michael Willhoite

Elsa Maxwell, Hostess with the Mostest

She was—let's face it—rather homely. Yet she was the most sought after woman in society. The grande dame of 20th century party-throwers, Elsa believed that amusing and provocative people helped make it great, but she left nothing to chance. *Loosen inhibitions! Deflate the stuffed shirts!* was her motto.

How about her "Come As You Were" party in Paris? "Were," meaning the moment the invitation, sent at all times of the day and night, was received. Guests arrived with toothbrushes, faces in mud packs, in pajamas, or shirts but no pants.

This is the kind of novelty that kept guests entertained. People actually paid to attend. One guest, who was visiting the conductor Toscanini's daughters, Wally and Wanda, wrote that when it became known that La Maxwell would be giving a special party, everyone was clamoring for an invitation. "I was one of the lucky ones," said the visiting guest. "This was to be fancy dress: men were to dress as women and vice-versa, in short, a transvestite affair. This being Venice, no one raised an eyebrow. Wally was vastly intrigued by the whole idea and promptly set about organizing costumes. She decreed that we should be dressed as rough sailors complete with 'six o'clock shadow' on our chins, while she herself stuck to the feminine gender, appearing as a convincing 'Madame' of a low class sea front brothel. One 'gentleman' really stood out from the crowd and that was Marlene Dietrich, flawless in top hat and tails."

That day is past, but any of us can throw a party that has a theme, a story or no purpose at all except fun. If there is a theme or purpose, choose a moment to make a point of it with your guests. This binds the group to the occasion and creates memories.

1   Flaunt your personal style, as Elsa advised.

You are your own celebrity. Enough already of the life vicarious. Half the celebrities out there aren't worthy of our devotion, much less time and attention. Cultivate what's individual about you. It will enrich your life.

Get Inspired

To help cultivate your style, keep a portfolio of magazine clippings or online file of ideas and settings for various occasions.

"The best parties are given by people who can't afford them. They must use imagination and ingenuity as substitutes for money... and the conclusive proof of it is my career."

- Elsa Maxwell

2   Have only as many guests as you can handle. Think of your space, budget, comfort zone and sanity.

Guest Rule

Asking to bring someone can be tricky for your host. Say sorry you're not free because you have a houseguest. Then it's up to the host.

Bianca Sharma, owner of the Amalfi Coast's beautiful boutique hotel, Monastero Santa Rosa, says that when she entertains privately she asks people to bring someone new whom she hasn't met. "I enjoy the opportunity to expand my relationships and to bring fresh conversations to the table."

3 Be sure to leave enough time to pull yourself together before guests arrive. But don't hit the wine bottle. Forget cleaning out closets or rearranging furniture. Walk the dog, walk the cat, walk anything.

"I strongly believe that how you live life every day is much more important than getting your house together for a special occasion."

- Suzanne Rheinstein
At Home: A Style for Today with Things from the Past

4 If you have a theme, you can thread it through every element from postage stamp to table setting, music to drinks. More than one table? Give them names, flagged on tent cards. It breaks the ice if you're seated at "The Real Housewives" table.

Get Inspired

A Houston host sent white cloths and colored markers in advance for a party to honor a man called Buck. The result? A cartoon gallery to tour before dinner. There's our hero holding onto a rocket for dear life at the Buck Rogers table; riding a bronco with hat and butt in the air at the Buckaroo table; presiding in the Oval Office at The Buck Stops Here. Only in Texas!

More Inspiration

One of the wackier themes was I Lost at Jeopardy, a party given by the wife of a losing entrant. Décor included posters of the great losers of history, Napoleon at Waterloo, Custer at his Last Stand. Their guitar-playing teenager entertained guests with a song he composed, "I'm a loser. Yeah!"

A theatrical producer in Manhattan commanded each guest—man, woman, child—to wear a white beard to a surprise 40th birthday party for a friend. When our buffed birthday boy walked into a room full of people looking as ancient as Abraham, he felt pretty smug. And decades younger.

A take on a movie theme was a Bette Davis party Peggy threw in Dallas. Guests had to dig up gossip about the glamour puss with the pack-a-day voice. Photos from her films adorned the table. After dinner, guests watched a video of The Old Maid *and did impersonations of Bette as Aunt Charlotte, Margot Channing* (All About Eve) *or Baby Jane* (What Ever Happened to...).

The Ultimate New York Party

While a lot of us love costumes, either to hide behind or the chance to become someone else for a night, mask and color themes are also fun and easier for guests to pull off. Truman Capote's famous Black and White Ball still sets the standard. What was it all about?

In 1966, with the huge success of *In Cold Blood*, Capote had money in his pocket and decided to throw the poshest event possible for his "friends." Just preparing the guest list created enormous buzz. Who was in and who was out? Invitations were so coveted and conferred such social validation that some who were not invited got the hell out of town. One woman told her husband she would kill herself if they were overlooked. Truman spread that far and wide.

The gala was held in the Grand Ballroom of New York's Plaza Hotel. For men, black tie and black masks. For women, white gowns, white masks and white fans. A drop dead spectacle. The food was Truman's favorites—chicken hash, see Recipes, and spaghetti and meatballs. But Taittinger Champagne flowed all evening.

Like so many things in life, it had its dark side. In the words of writer John Knowles, "Don't you think Truman sat there in Monroeville, Alabama, when he was about ten...strange little outcast even in his own house, and said that someday he would hire the most beautiful ballroom in New York City and he would have the most elegant and famous people in the world there?"

And he did. Frank Sinatra, Mia Farrow, Babe Paley, the Alfred Gwynne Vanderbilts, the Nelson Rockefellers, the Maharajah and Maharani of Jaipur, Norman Mailer, Lee Radziwill, Lauren Bacall. Henry Ford, Henry Fonda, Gloria Guinness, Andy Warhol. Anyone who counted in Hollywood, industry, publishing, art, fashion, finance, society. Not to mention the most powerful woman in the country, guest of honor Kay Graham, owner and president of The Washington Post.

In giving the Party of the Century, Truman Capote "made 500 friends and 15,000 enemies."

We don't advise making enemies but in case we do, here's a toast: Champagne to my real friends, real pagne to my cham friends.

Get Inspired

Why not try a modern twist on the black and white theme? Dress code white and everything else, even toilet tissue, black. Blackjack the game, black drinks with Blavod British vodka on black lacquer trays, dishes of black jellybeans and olives, caviar and/or black bean paste on black bread. Servers, if you have them, dressed in black.

More Inspiration

Or theme around games—mahjong, pool, Scrabble, bridge, Texas hold 'em poker—remember the "Desperate Housewives" morning poker party? Give inexpensive prizes that relate.

Risque Business. Put the name of a person with "a past" on a 4x6 card (Benedict Arnold, Madame Bovary, Bernie Madoff) and pin on the back of each guest. Only yes or no questions allowed in discovering who s/he is. Am I a female? Have I been in jail? Do I live in the neighborhood? In the 18th century?

5 Don't outdress or upstage your guests. Cleavage leads to cleavers, save it for clubbing. An American Idol wannabe? No one can stop you singing your lungs out but they don't have to come back.

"It was difficult not to look at Miss Orrincourt's diamonds. They were a sort of visual faux pas, which no amount of blameless small-talk could shout down."

                                                              - Ngaio Marsh

6 A Classic Roman Rule about numbers for dinner: No more than the Muses (nine) nor less than the Graces (three). Might this have something to do with how many togas could fit on the banquet couches?

That other classic, Emily Post, ruled that 12 is maximum served smoothly at a sit-down dinner without help.

New Rule

Unless drinks are wine only and food is self-serve—or you're a real whiz at this—12 is heartburn. Enlist help if more than eight for a sit-down dinner or a dozen for drinks.

If you go the self-serve route, you can put everything out at once, including desserts. It used to be called a smorgasbord. Let guests find seats or eat standing up. It's casual, people can even start with sweets if they want. What you lose is the intimacy that comes with everyone at the same table, having the same conversation, laughing at the same jokes.

Tip

Hiring help doesn't have to break the bank. The menu of courses at your local college may include cooking and/or bartending. The local theatre may direct you to actors who moonlight. Still less expensive than going to a restaurant.

Guest Rule

You don't have to reciprocate in kind but you do have to reciprocate.

"For the millions of us who live glued to computer keyboards at work and TV monitors at home, food may be more than entertainment. It may be the only sensual experience left."

– Barbara Ehrenreich

CHAPTER TWO

Gathering Guests:
Invitations, Occasions and Hours

Gathering guests isn't necessarily as artless as it may seem. Decisions about whom to invite, the chemistry among them, reciprocity (whom you may want versus whom you owe), settling on a date that is convenient for you and your guests, dietary issues. These are some of the considerations.

On the other hand, what could be easier than a gathering for two? Or more romantic?

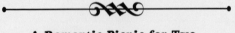

A Romantic Picnic for Two

When we showed young Vicky the description of a picnic in *The Butler's Guide* by Stanley Ager and Fiona St. Aubyn, she said, "You must be kidding. Why wouldn't you just go to a deli and buy a couple of sandwiches!"

Well, you wouldn't because *The Butler*, while acknowledging that appetite is not the most important aspect of a romantic picnic, does insist that the food must be of a high quality. Not to mention the presentation.

We might not follow everything *The Butler* prescribes, but it is definitely fun to read about his idea of a picnic as we conjure a meadow in the incomparably beautiful English countryside, where we're driven through the hedgerows in an open roadster and where we seem never to be bothered by such petty annoyances as flies or mosquitos. Only a few benign sheep nodding at us nearby. There is always the threat of rain, of course, which even the most competent butler can do nothing about.

Once we get past recommendations on food that is appropriate for the occasion and advice on how best to wrap and transport it—all of it in those peerless tones that convey the notion that this is obviously how it's done and how could anyone possibly think otherwise—the menu in fact is rather simple.

Soup, the suggestion of a lobster bisque, which "tickles up the palette." Turtle soup is also mentioned! And the point made that a thick broth is hardly romantic.

Several patés with a baguette or toasts.

Salad, being mindful of the color that radishes will add. Ending with, what else? Strawberries and cream. Though apples or oranges are alternatives, with an admonition about polishing the apples.

An ordinary bottle of plonk is not romantic. Without question you will bring china plates. You might even go out and buy two special ones in order to remember this outing. If the romance curdles, you have the option of throwing the china against the wall.

As for cutlery, only a direct quote would do *The Butler* justice· "It is tempting to take silver, but silver scratches easily, and I wouldn't want to see it lying on the ground or have the worry that a piece might be lost. Sadly, I think one must take stainless steel."

More sadly by far is that we don't have anyone like Stanley Ager around to plan and prepare our romantic picnic and pack it up in a smart looking hamper. As entertainments go, however, this really is one of the simplest. The payoff? A romance, or at least a pleasant afternoon in the park.

If not, there's always the deli. Say hello to Vicky if she happens to be there.

Invitations

Whether using paper, evites or texting, don't forget the basics: occasion, place, date, time, RSVP info and dress code, if there is one (black tie, costume or, if no jeans, casual but smart). For a cocktail party include "until" time. This gives you at least a shot at closing the door on stragglers before sun-up!

Bravo to those who specify "no gifts" for adult celebrations.

7   Do not send invitations too far in advance. It puts people on the spot, allowing for no way out.

Guest Rule
It's rude to ignore an RSVP unless the invitation says "regrets only." Dragging your heels is irritating to a host and leads to the suspicion you're waiting for a better offer to come along. And how can the host calculate quantities? For a party that is catered, she will be charged per guest, show or no show.

8   Give guests up to a half hour window to arrive for cocktail parties, where you're standing politely at the door to greet. Then you may leave your post.

If dinner follows your allotted cocktail hour, seat your guests and proceed no matter who is late or a no-show.

Guest Rule
Showing up early for a party is a one-way ticket to Siberia, take a hike.

If you are invited for dinner, remember your host has timed the food so honor her indicated time. You have a margin of 10-15 minutes.

9   Inviting someone at the last minute to fill in? Say so, you're not fooling anyone.

Old Guest Rule

You do not refuse a last minute invitation if you're free.

New Rule

If you'd rather stay home in your jammies, it's okay by us.

Get Inspired

For a holiday entertainment in Boston, where a pianist was the featured attraction, invitations were affixed to little red pianos.

A savvy realtor threw her own housewarming in the form of a garden party. Invitations asked guests to "bring something from your garden to mine"—a perennial reminder for her of an evening under the stars with a constellation of friends.

Ted Dawson

Occasions and Hours

We all know basic timing for various occasions. Nevertheless this may serve as a handy guide.

10   Rules of thumb on timing

Breakfast: *9 to 11*
Brunch: *11 to 1 or 12 to 2*

Tip
Invest in a smoothie and/or cappuccino or Nespresso machine.

Lunch: *12:30 to 3 or 1 to 3:30*
This is not just for "ladies who lunch." It's a good entertaining option for us all because hours are limited, leaving the rest of the weekend free.

Get Inspired
An informal lunch hosted by an artist whose house and studio are set amid the rolling hills and meadows of Columbia County, north of Manhattan, featured a richly flavored mushroom soup. He ladled it from a blue Le Creuset casserole on the stove. A vase of yellow flowers rested on a cutting board on the next burner- nice touch! We went back for prosciutto, breads, olive paste and other spreads. Dessert was red berries with a mix of whipped, sour cream and crème fraiche in white square bowls, a work of art and reminiscent of the garden party in Neuilly we tell you about later.

Old Rule for Teas: *between 3 and 5*
New Rule: *anytime from 2 on*

Teas are featured at some of the best hotels and clubs, usually high tea, meaning the whole shebang from Champagne to finger sandwiches to desserts. It follows that we're increasingly hosting them at home.

Get Inspired
A Japanese "tea ceremony" with bamboo mats, square plates, han-

dle-less cups. Rice crackers, finger sandwiches of smoked or sushi salmon or other seafood, teriyaki chicken or shrimp.

Or for diehard romantics, a Victorian Tea Party with your collection of cups and saucers, paper fans, doilies, silver tea service. Start with small crust-less sandwiches of cucumber, watercress, egg salad, smoked salmon, followed by scones and clotted cream (substitute lightly sweetened whipped cream with a touch of sour cream added).

Cocktail Party: *not before 6:30 or 7 during the week in most urban areas but as early as 5 on weekends; community custom dictates*

Dinner Party: *6 on, or even before if you're an early bird special*
Dessert Party: *9 to 11 or 10 to midnight*

Open House/Big Bash: *usually a weekend afternoon for four or five hours*

An impromptu: *anytime*

Get Inspired
A host in Seaside, Florida, says: Weather's great, let's have a shrimp peel. He throws a package of Cajun seasoning in with the boiling shrimp—two minutes tops!—deli coleslaw on the side, hot sauce, rolls of paper towels. No one can hide behind a façade when they're peelin' and dunkin' shrimp with their fingers. Almost as easy is shrimp scampi- you just have to do the peeling. See Recipes.

Tips-When to Invite
Weddings, bar and bat mitzvahs, sweet sixteens, quinceñaeras: *six to eight weeks.*
Most other occasions: *ten days in advance.*

Holiday season, when calendars fill up: *two weeks or more.*
Casual get-togethers: *a few days, even hours if you can pull it off.*

Save "save-the-date" cards for the trash heap, say some, but it is practical when inviting people from long distances or when calendars are crowded at holiday time.

"Amuse 'em, feed 'em or shock 'em."

- Oscar Wilde

We try for at least two out of three.

CHAPTER THREE

Visuals:
Setting the Scene, Lighting, Flowers

Marcelline's Memory of a Dinner Party in Bangkok

Bangkok, Venice of Asia, laced with klongs. Tropical, monsoon season charged with drama, dazzling the senses with sounds and colors so exotic they could never be imagined, even in an opium dream. The land of *The King and I* and *mai pen rai*, three little words that cover any part of laid-back from let's not worry about it now to let's not worry about it ever.

The city's pleasures were subtle then, rounds of parties, outdoors usually, despite the mosquitoes in attendance, and curry lunches on Sunday on porches under slow moving fans. An invitation from the Lewises was treasured, this time for dinner with parents visiting from Vancouver. Fran and Tim wore their wealth lightly. They were fun, and they had style. Humor and generosity, too, and as fabulous as their parties were, we never felt we had to reciprocate in kind. A bottle of anything imported was a month's rent on our little house in Soi Ruam Rudee.

It was after sundown, a little cooler, when the flowers, the orchids and frangipani and roses and jasmine and others whose names we would never learn, have time to recover from the withering heat and once again rise to fill the night with their fragrance. Tree frogs and other creatures chirped joyously, punctuated from time to time by the deep croak of a tokay from a nearby klong. Paper lanterns hung from low-lying tree branches and lined the walks and terraces, winking like thousands of fireflies. They flashed a bit brighter with the briefest stirring of air, perhaps no more than the whisper of a woman's dress as she passed by.

The staff, barefoot, in white cotton blouses or shirts over sarongs, moved among us on the terrace with dishes of spiced nuts and other nibbles, before guiding us into the garden. Profusions of gladioli, salmon-colored and standing high in Chinese vases along the paths or cut low for the tables covered with cloths glowing golden in the reflection of the lanterns and the goblets of wine already poured. Our first course was smoked salmon, flown in, fanned out on china echoing the color scheme. I haven't seen anything since quite so harmoniously beautiful.

Setting the Scene

Think about décor as adding to the fun, beginning with something as simple as a bunch of greens tied with raffia and hung on the front door.

Get Inspired

Artist Polly McCaffrey, who has a house in the Hudson Valley, follows the seasons by forcing showy branches of forsythia, quince or cherry, cutting cool ornamental grasses in summer, leaves in autumn, pines or holly in winter. What a dramatic greeting! Something we always talk about as we drive up: What will it be this time?

11 Warm things up in winter and cool them down in summer. Light a fire in the fireplace if you have one and if you don't, use a video. Use sherbet colors in summer, put a parasol or vase of flowers in the fireplace.

12 Pamper your guests in the bath or powder room—a vase with a single flower, fancy soaps, guest towels. Go the distance and add aspirin, powder, hand cream, breath freshener.

13 Bubala's Rule: Get rid of clutter so people don't stumble and tchotkes tumble.

Lighting

"Candlelight makes everyone look beautiful, and if people feel like they look nice, they're going to have a good time."

\- Event designer David Beahm

14 Keep it intimate but don't leave guests in the dark, eating their napkin rings. Bright lights, however, are the kiss of death. You don't want your party described like "a high school dance" as overheard recently.

15 Vampire Rule: No candlelight before dark.

Ted Drawson

New Rule

Why not? We like candlelight whenever the mood strikes. It adds mystery and romance and nothing should get in the way of either.

Tips

One way to set the stage: Line walkway or steps with luminarias, decorative paper bags filled with sand to hold candles. Go online and order. The effect is magic.

Candles used outside should always be protected for safety. Candles on the table inside might drip if room is drafty—or maybe it's that windbag you invited! A good way to scrape up wax is with the edge of a credit card.

Put colorful paper shades over light fixtures with low wattage bulbs. Or even burlap tied over the bulb to cast a soft glow.

16 Never put scented candles on the table with food. Guests may be allergic and certainly the food is. Ever been to a dinner party where everything tasted like lavender?

17 Safety Rule: The snugger the fit, the longer the burn, the safer the guests.

18 Test wicks by lighting them in advance to make sure none is faulty. You don't want to be scrounging for a replacement at the eleventh hour. Also, candles will flame immediately when re-lit.

19 Candles must be above or below eye level or your guests will be deer in the headlights.

Old Rule

Candles must be slightly taller than the candleholders.

New Rule

Candles can be any height as long as they are about equal and follow the eye level rule.

20 Direct lights are harsh, unless you have a dimmer; indirect lights are soft. Pink and yellow bulbs are the most flattering and send everyone home a little bit enchanted if not in love.

21 Chandeliers should hang 30 inches above the table to provide enough light but not block sightlines. If ceiling is higher than eight feet, the distance can increase.

Flowers

22 Cupid's Rule: Flowers should not interfere with sightlines either. Let guests see each other—and flirt—across the table.

23 Two colors, safe. Three? Sorry, unless you're a floral artist. More than three? Cheesy. And give yourself plenty of time to fuss with them. If a special occasion, hire it done.

In Downton Abbey fashion, a footman in London recounted that for a special party he would find out from the lady's maid what color gown the hostess was to wear. If flowers weren't being brought up from the country by train, he would go to Covent Garden early in the morning to buy matching blooms.

"Buy your flowers at the grocery store, take the tacky stuff out, put the rest in a pretty vase and it will look like you've gone straight to the garden and picked them."

- Dallas Socialite Peggy Riggs

Get Inspired

Line a row of small vases—all glass, all pottery, etc.—with a stem in each down the middle of the table. Since they're small, you can use a variety of colors.

Author/illustrator Emily Arnold McCully floats daylilies from her garden for a centerpiece, stems removed, rather than predictable roses. Or mix holly and hydrangea—the deep green and sharp edges of the one play off the fullness and softness of the other.

24 As with candles, never put strong-scented flowers like Casablanca lilies on the table, for the same reasons. They season the food and you could end up with sneezers.

An example of every rule is meant to be broken, we love this idea from Charlotte Moss about lemon verbena. In the garden or on the window sill with some good light, it grows easily and fast, and lemon is the favorite scent of Americans.

"The gentle aroma of an infusion, its calming, refreshing, and relaxing effect, or simply pinching a leaf to release its fragrance are just a couple of ways this delicate plant will reward you."

- Charlotte Moss

Guest Rule

Show up with something but please no flowers or fresh foods, forcing your host to drop everything and figure out what to do with them. Send flowers the next day. If bringing wine, put your name on it to be remembered. The host will appreciate it too.

"Resist the temptation to make your table setting the living embodiment of your ego."

- Craig Claiborne

25 Make the table a feast for the eye and tell a story. Think stage setting, a painting, a fairy tale, something from your travels.

Tip

For ideas check out Colin Cowie's Dinner After Dark.

Get Inspired

Use a sequined flapper dress or a shawl draped across the center of the table to add zing. These are easily found nowadays with the proliferation of estate sales, vintage clothing shops and second time around stores.

A centerpiece with your collection of rock crystal, old pharmacy vessels, treasured sea shells. Don't be tentative.

Put jellybeans, silvered almonds or pieces of candied ginger on the table in your grandmother's collection of demitasse cups. Or buy customized M&M's. How sweet is that? Even limited to two lines at eight characters per line, they make a fun party favor. You can pick colors, too, to keep within your theme.

If a small crowd, put a small something on the plate, people love surprises. Popular in the 1920's, favors fell into disfavor, enjoyed a return engagement in the 60's, and have gone in and out of fashion since. We're noticing a comeback.

More Inspiration

If celebrants at a Beverly Hills lawn party weren't already "fans" of the honoree, a noted interior designer, they became so when hand fans bearing his likeness were passed around on a sizzling afternoon. Overheated guests refreshed themselves and took home a cool memento.

One famous annual party is the post-Oscars Vanity Fair *shindig in Beverly Hills hosted by editor-in-chief Graydon Carter. He recalls: "Over the years we've had old-fashioned cigarette girls, engraved Zippo lighters, lollipops with movie stars' faces on them, cookies glazed with* Vanity Fair *covers, and In-N-Out burgers for folks arriving late and famished. Guests seem to love these little novelties. They also seem to love the various room accessories. Pewter ashtrays, which were inspired by one I saw in a Terence Conran restaurant, and which weigh as much as bowling balls, disappear by the dozens each year. Once we had lamps with shades featuring stills from Oscar-nominated movies. They vanished, too."*

CHAPTER FOUR

The Cocktail Party:
Quantities, A Well-Stocked Bar, Finger Food

The Great Gatsby

All of us have been invited to one of the best parties of all, one that came from the imagination of F. Scott Fitzgerald. It was given by Jay Gatsby at his mansion in West Egg on Long Island in the vain hope that he could win back Daisy, the illusion at the end of the dock across the water.

What is it about a gathering that drifts onto lawn and garden? It is suggestive of magic and charm. It speaks of summer pleasures, of flower-scented evenings filled with light and laughter, the promise that it cannot end. In bygone days, a garden historian has noted, this was the one place where a little privacy could be found. Perhaps half the population was conceived along the primrose path.

"There was music from my neighbor's house through the summer nights. In his blue gardens men and girls came and went like moths among the whisperings and the champagne and the stars...

"The last swimmers have come in from the beach now and are dressing upstairs; the cars from New York are parked five deep in the drive, and already the halls and salons and verandas are gaudy with primary colors, and hair shorn in strange new ways, and shawls beyond the dreams of Castile...."

- The Great Gatsby by F. Scott Fitzgerald

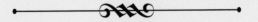

Cocktail parties are the easiest form of hospitality, not least because guests come expecting to entertain themselves. Once launched, there's nothing left for you to do but enjoy yourself, and nothing ensures success more than a host who's having fun. For small gatherings, you can serve the first drink, then suggest people help themselves to seconds. Just make sure the bar is accessible.

"I am drinking stars."

- Dom Perignon

Why not reach for them? A party promising Champagne is all the entertainment and glamour some of us need. There's nothing wrong with prosecco, cava or crémant for a more affordable bubble.

26 Don't cast a wide net unless it's a party that's big enough to absorb both business and social friends. But, friends can be a wonderful buffer with colleagues or clients or fractious family, helping to take the spotlight and pressure off you.

Tip
A cocktail gathering must have critical mass to feel festive—in most rooms this will be at least 12 people. To ensure that you attain it, invite 16 to allow for dropouts.

27 To grease social wheels, invite some people who've already met each other but not so many as to form cliques. The best host in the world cannot separate the inseparable.

28 Fawning Alert: Don't do this over some guests more than others. It's ungracious, and people do notice.

Guest Rule
If you have a mishap—usually a broken glass—insist on paying for it.

It's not about the money, it's courtesy. Up to you if you want to send a check or slip a twenty in an envelope. The gracious host plays down any such accident, sparing the guest embarrassment, but we find nothing wrong if that check is cashed. It may seem petty but you have no idea whether it was Crate and Barrel or Baccarat. If the latter, you've at least made a down payment on a little good will.

Tip

The best hosts delight in finding connections among guests—those famous "six degrees of separation." If you're not going to help people meet each other, why bother bringing them together?

29 Use only votive or contained candles for a cocktail party and keep them out of reach because people gesture when storytelling, especially when drinking. A friend once found her favorite Armani jacket smoldering from a nearby naked candle. That's a host taking atmosphere too far.

30 If serving wine only and for just a few guests, don't be stingy. Break open the good stuff. Not so important in a crowd when wine won't be the focus, but that isn't license to pour rotgut either. Moderately priced wines will do fine.

Tips

No straight up cocktails without a bartender. The ritual of the shaker and chilling the glasses just takes too much time.

College kids may leap at the chance to earn extra money bartending. Or check the Web for a party staff service in your area.

Pick a signature drink like Aperol, an Italian aperitif that tastes of orange rind and spice, one that bartenders world-round have embraced. Serve on the rocks; with grapefruit juice and the French liqueur St.

Germain; or in place of Campari in a Negroni.

An easy way to serve drinks is to make pitchers in advance: Sangria, Cosmos, Bloody Marys, Margaritas, Mimosas or Mojitos.

Or try this holiday idea from Bacardi and Chef Jonathan Lindenauer: Punch, made with fresh juices, citrus slices and Bacardi Gold. Nothing says party like a classic punch bowl. If a crowd, have two or even three of them. You don't want guests having to line up to get a drink. Truffled popcorn is an ideal companion, a luxe take on everyone's favorite treat. Drizzle melted butter flavored with a touch of black truffle oil and tossed with a little grated parmesan and salt.

31 You must offer something non-alcoholic, so make it appealing. A favorite of ours is a pitcher of pomegranate juice with club soda and slices of lemon or lime. There are also good non-alcoholic beers on the market.

32 Finger food must be just that—manageable with fingers. See Recipes.

33 You need four paper or two linen cocktail napkins per person per hour. Fewer if cocktail plates are used.

Tip

Look for vintage cocktail napkins at the next estate sale. Many were printed with amusing aphorisms or toasts. A recent find were the so-called sayings of Confucius. "Man who go in cheap restaurant for good steak, sometimes get bum steer" and "Man who spend time at racetrack often find wife a nag."

Guest Rule

If invitation specifies an "until" time, you must observe it, with a lee-

way of perhaps 20 minutes.

"What is your host's purpose in having a party? Surely not for you to enjoy yourself; if that were their sole purpose, they'd have simply sent Champagne and women over to your place by taxi."

- P.J. O'Rourke

Drink Quantities

34 Bartenders Rule: A pound of ice for every six people, but a pound per person when also chilling bottles.

The Big Chill

Fastest way to chill white wine and Champagne is in a bucket with ice and water, 20 minutes—adding some water makes it easier to tuck in the wine. For beer, 15 minutes.

In the freezer, 45 minutes. Yes, you can. A few say it diminishes the quality. We say, nonsense. Only reason not to is the chance you'll forget it's in there. Set a timer!

In the fridge, 2 hours

Tip

Don't serve wine and beer igloo cold. This compromises flavor.

35 For each guest per hour
- *one to one and a half drinks*
- *one to one and a half glasses of wine*
- *one bottle of beer*

For each guest for a two-hour cocktail party
- *6 ounces spirits*
- *half a bottle of wine*
- *two to three bottles/cans for each beer drinker*

Tips

How to calculate the split between wine and beer drinkers? If you think it's about even, buy enough of each for 60 percent of your crowd.

And the split between white and red wine drinkers? Anybody's guess. Have enough of each, figuring this won't be your last party and you'll use what's left over.

For spirits drinkers, stock the bar with at least the basics: gin, vodka, Scotch.

Yields

A 750 ml bottle of distilled spirits = 16 drinks on a 1.5 ounce pour
A liter = 22-23 drinks
A 1.75 liter bottle = about 40 drinks
A standard bottle of wine, 750 ml = 5 glasses
A standard bottle of Champagne = 8-10 flutes
A magnum of Champagne, or two bottles = 16-20 flutes

Or, skip the mundane magnum and imbibe Biblically: from a Jeroboam, Rehoboam, Methusaleh, Mordechai, Salmanazar, Balthazar, Nebuchadnezzar and the granddaddy of all, Melchizedek, standing four feet tall and equal to 40 standard bottles! All are names of actual Champagne sizes. Was this an example of medieval monks' marketing technique? As to whether these super-size-me bottles deliver the fizz, most experts say there's no real difference.

A Well-Stocked Bar

Vodka, gin, Scotch, bourbon, tequila, vermouth, Cointreau for Cosmopolitans, or whatever ingredient for the rage drink of the moment. Add rum in the summer months. If the bar is self-serve, or will be after the first drink, consider buying one liter bottles. Not as cost effective but easier for your guests to handle.

Checklist

- ☐ Both red and white wine
- ☐ Beer from microbrews are generally superior and you support local-businesses
- ☐ Flat and sparkling water or soda, tonic, OJ, cranberry or pomegranate juice, colas, both regular and diet; diet drinks are unhealthy but some people still request them
- ☐ Worcestershire and Tabasco sauces
- ☐ Lemons, limes, green olives for traditional martinis, celery sticks if serving Bloody Marys, though we prefer limes
- ☐ Cocktail shaker but remember our advice: no straight up cocktails without a bartender
- ☐ Corkscrew, bottle opener
- ☐ Ice bucket and tongs, small spoon
- ☐ Jigger - measures 1½ ounces
- ☐ Small cutting board and knife
- ☐ Lemon/lime squeezer
- ☐ Bar towels - find something colorful or clever
- ☐ Cocktail napkins
- ☐ Nuts or similar bar snack

36 Have half again as many glasses as guests. People often put drinks down and forget where.

You need wine, lowball and highball glasses. And flutes for Champagne, prosecco or cava, if serving.

Why bother with flutes? Because bubbles hustle and flow right up to the rim of the glass where they form a collar, collerette, that deliciously tingles the nose and palate. In coupes, those wide-mouthed, shallow glasses, the bubbles rise a bit, then disperse and deflate.

"If it makes you happy to drink it out of a water cup or a cool little Italian country glass, go for it. Just drink and be happy."

- Seth Box, Moët Hennessy USA

Finger Food Quantities

37

Cheaper by the Dozen Rule:

12 bite-size hors d'oeuvres per guest over two hours.

Two per person of each different hors d'oeuvre served.

For cheeses and dips, one ounce equals a bite.

Calorie Counter's Rule

The harder the cheese, the lesser the fat, the fewer the calories.

If the cocktail party is scheduled on the late side, that is, during hours that are customarily dinnertime (say 6:30 to 8:30), count on up to 20 hors d'oeuvres per person. Many guests will plan to have heavy hors d'oeuvres and call it a night.

If a light dinner follows, plan on 5-7 bites per person for an hour.

If a more substantial dinner follows, a bowl of nuts, a dish of olives and one canapé, such as smoked salmon on a cracker, will suffice.

38 The more formal the occasion, the less people eat.

39 Round up, not down.

40 Increase variety and heft for holiday or other large parties that last longer.

Tip

For large parties where people drive, consider valet parking. Give the job to a couple of responsible teenagers.

41 For parties that will go long, provide coffee. You may have legal liability if guests drive intoxicated. And you won't have to ring a bell signaling it's time to go home or, like the husband of a friend, put on pajamas and parade through the room like the ghost of Christmas past.

Serving sweets at the end helps too.

Starbucks says a pound of coffee yields 45 8-oz cups. Your serving size will likely be closer to six ounces so adjust accordingly. Many take it black but have two quarts of milk on hand.

42 Nursery Rule: cocktail parties are not occasions for children unless peeking from the top of the stairs. The same goes for pets.

CHAPTER FIVE

Dining In and Out:
Simple Suppers, Short Cuts,
Sit-Down Dinner Party

How the French Do It

One of the best dinner parties Peggy ever attended was in a *petit jardin* outside Paris, at the house of Michèle and Claude Sachs.

It could well have been one of those sun-bleached resort towns on the Mediterranean like Beaulieu, the air was so fragrant. Strolling the paths among timeworn statuary and stone planters filled with red geraniums, we sipped apéritifs. The butler for the evening—the postman in his day job—passed canapés of foie gras on toast rounds.

We were eight, including a friend from college days, now a professor. She and I had spent the better part of the afternoon getting "done up" because we knew the French women would be drop-dead chic. And they were. Michèle, who had been an exchange student with my family, was the same weight now as then. In a simple white suit she was a double for Ingrid Bergman in *Casablanca*. Claudine wore a pink Chanel knit dress and jeweled belt designed to call attention to her unfairly small waist.

We sat for dinner at 10 o'clock. Goat cheese croustade was followed by Poulet Rôti aux Senteurs, with pommes frites and haricots verts, accompanied by wonderful wines, including a Médoc. Dessert? Simplicity itself, four kinds of red berries in glass bowls with crème Chantilly. Conversation turned to politics. Along with religion, it's usually a no-

no dinner topic. Not so in France, where it can be discussed in a polite and unimpassioned way.

We drank the last of the wine as darkness descended. White irises immersed in a square vase on the table became luminescent. As did the white candles—two in Baccarat and two in cheapo imports shaped like huge upside down Champagne flutes. Michèle prowls the lobbies of Paris' luxury hotels and copycats the latest look. We had Cognac and café filtre in the antiques-filled salon, an Edith Piaf recording in the background. It was two o'clock in the morning when we said bon nuit, wondering when we would see each other again.

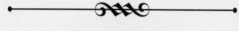

The Dinner Party

It's a joyful gathering with friends so let's not worry if we can't channel a chic French hostess. Cooking behind closed doors for a formal dinner party is becoming as obsolete as the dodo. Fun and casual is more the norm, with everyone gathered around the bar or in the kitchen pitching in.

Home will always be inviting, no matter your circumstances. As a friend put it in an email, "If you prefer a restaurant, that's fine too, but it's more relaxed at home. Plus we can have more time and be less well behaved."

While some declare that the dinner party is dead, we say long live the dinner party. Brooklynite Karen Mordechai started Sunday Suppers because there's nothing better than sitting around the table with family and friends. She contends that even the best restaurants don't approximate the intimate spirit of eating at home. Her gatherings have been so successful people now subscribe at more than $100 per person. As soon as the next supper is posted online, it sells out. "People wanted that old school dinner party feel," Mordechai told *The New York Times.*

"The idea of cooking for others is not something that is going to die."
                                    - Miss Manners (Judith Martin)

Sharing a meal is the heart and soul of fellowship, a ritual as ancient as the Biblical breaking of bread or, as we've said, probably as far back as the cave dwellers. When we ourselves didn't have three spoons between us, crammed into apartments to share the rent, we still had our little dinners, Oscar nights, birthdays, engagements or break-up celebrations. The menus may not have won prizes, but we made it a rule to pour a decent wine and serve decent food, no matter how plain or how limited our ability at the stove. As we climbed our respective career and marital ladders, this has remained a constant. We will always have the memories and enduring friendships to prove it.

Some of us enjoy serving food by the pool, around the grill or at a buffet in a tent on the lawn, at tables in the garage or wherever we find room. We know someone in Manhattan who managed a dinner for 16 in his studio apartment. You don't have to be totally restricted by space.

Simple Suppers and Short Cuts

Nothing could be simpler than supper with friends around the kitchen table—burgers, a dead easy pot pie or hearty soup with bread and cheese, see Recipes, a bottle or two of whatever-buck chuck from Trader Joe's. Or this idea from *The New York Times* for an easy meal: scooped out baked potatoes stuffed with a choice of chili or mushroom ragout and a salad, see Recipes, and you're done. Just being in the kitchen says casual. No great distance to travel from stove to table. Bar and wine on the counter, everyone helps themselves.

Potluck is the greatest time saver of all. It requires some organizing so you don't end up with...well, more variations on that baked potato. On the other hand you've got an instant theme!

Or start out with a theme. A party in Scottsdale celebrated Cinco de

Mayo with fajitas on the grill. Guests were assigned to bring the rest: tortillas, shredded cheese, sour cream, salsa, chopped romaine lettuce, black beans, rice and flan for dessert.

Tip

Consult Ina Garten's new cookbook, Make It Ahead.

Five Easy Pieces: Shortcuts on Serving

Even at a sit-down dinner, you can signal casual by passing food in the roasting pans.

Or as a friend has done, put a casserole of coq au vin with a dish of parsley potatoes in the center of the table. We like chicken cacciatore with bacon for a somewhat easier dish, and who doesn't like bacon? Leave it out if you don't. See Recipes.

Or, as other friends did recently, invite people to the pots on the stove, in this case one with bouillabaisse, one with rice. For a one pot presentation, skip the rice and serve with crusty bread or cornbread. See Recipes.

If everything is room temperature, plate an hour or so in advance.

In grilling season, all bets are off. Yet another reason to welcome spring in the north.

43 Ina Garten's Rule: Cook no more than two courses: purchase or assemble the other course(s).

Short Cuts: Doctoring deli and other ruses

- Make your own sauce for pre-cooked chicken breasts with butter and mustard, wine and/or broth and mushrooms.
- Do a special glaze for a ham, pre-cooked of course, with bourbon or rum, brown sugar and mustard.
- Spice up packaged slaw with bottled ranch dressing, adding lime juice

and cumin.

- Buy packaged greens and dress with a mix of soy, vegetable oil, lime juice, garlic and ginger and slice leftover, or quickly pan-grilled, steak on top for an almost instant Thai salad. Add red peppers if you want.

- Sprinkle fresh herbs on a prepared pasta dish from your local gourmet shop and grate fresh parmesan over it.

- Embellish ice cream with a hot brandied chocolate sauce topped with finely chopped walnuts for "homemade" hot fudge sundaes.

Cheating with a Chef

Easiest of all, just hire a chef! Or ask a friend who loves cooking. You're in charge of the drinks and shopping for the wine. What's more luxurious than being catered to in your own home? It's everything going out has going for it, but you're settling back on the couch, whatever the weather, nobody's counting the cost of that second drink or the wine—never again that sinking feeling when you get the inflated bill because Ms. Piggy turned the evening into her personal bail-out. And tasting new dishes is so much fun. Especially when someone else is in charge of how they turn out. Cleaning up too! Bliss.

The Sit-Down Dinner

The most gracious form of entertaining and in many ways the most satisfying for you and your guests is the sit-down dinner. It fosters conversation and laughter. Many of the rules that follow relate to this ultimate expression of hospitality.

44 Our Rule: Dinner for eight at 8 (cocktails at 7) is the best of all possible worlds.

- It's intimate, yet enough for lively conversation but not so many that

your attention is pulled every which way
- Most of us have service for eight
- Many recipes are scaled for four and easily doubled. Caution: ingredients and cooking times are not always increased in a logical way so multiplying can be tricky business.

"7 for 8" is the succinct way Londoners express our rule. Guests are in no doubt about when to show up for a drink and when to expect food on the table.

For ultimate simplicity, serve your dinner for eight "family" style, meaning all the main course dishes, which you have chosen for ease in serving this way, are on the table for guests to help themselves.

Guest Rule
Don't eat and run, linger about an hour after dinner.

When having six or more for dinner, use place cards or at least have a seating plan. This is so reassuring to guests, who don't have the awkwardness of choosing where to sit. You don't want them settling beside best friends instead of mingling. Plus you have a chance to seat people for best matches—maybe that fix-up you always wanted to orchestrate.

45

Tips

Place cards can add an element of fun and reinforce the theme. A sneak peek at a place card also helps guests with the names of their dinner companions.

Buy tented cards at a stationery store and you won't need holders. Or create your own: use wine corks and just cut a crevice lengthwise with a sharp knife. Or slip a card through a colorful grosgrain ribbon tied around a sprig of rosemary.

Get Inspired

Some use place cards as favors, putting names in miniature frames, for example. Or tucking them in small pots of clover or wheatgrass.

Peggy once found beautiful vintage place cards at an estate sale, one of those dollar bags that can contain almost anything. Decorated with pen and ink drawings of birds with real feathers, the cards had been used, the names old-fashioned—Cecil and Victoria, Penelope and Graham, Percival, and so on. At a dinner party for a friend, she put the cards around the table and told her guests to assume the character of the name on their place card. Much merriment ensued.

46 Tippler's Rule: Cocktail hour before dinner should be just that... one hour.

"Run a taut ship, not a tight ship."

- Kay Corinth

How many of us have waited the endless "hour," wondering if dinner will appear before we're too stupefied to get to the table? If it's the host who's tipsy, now's the time for an attack of the vapors and a quick exit. Go for a pizza. And don't forget to send aspirin with the flowers next day.

Tip
A smart trick: "invite" yourself for an hour earlier than your guests and you'll all show up on time. There is nothing appealing about frantic.

Guest Prep Rule
Come with an amusing—but short—tale to tell. The more you contribute, the better time you'll have.

Zen and food: Remember, the journey of a thousand meals begins with one recipe.

Michael Pollan has written and spoken eloquently on the importance of cooking, not just for health but our overall sense of happiness and wellbeing. We're not suggesting this is all wonderful fun. What we are suggesting is that from time to time it is so worth it, not least because you control what you eat and can choose organic produce, antibiotic-free meats and chicken that hasn't had a cholrine bath. The trick is deciding not to be burdened, that you will devote a certain number of hours and enjoy it. The message must resonate, given proliferation of farmers markets, popularity of gardening and Community Supported Agriculture, not to mention investment in the slow food movement.

47 Some say planning is the secret of life. It's a courtesy to let guests know what to expect, even reciting the menu for them. Planning is also the key to effortless entertaining. Choose foods to be held in a warm oven or served at room temperature. If one dish is left to finish while guests are there, make sure it takes you away from them no more than ten minutes.

"At a dinner party, one should eat wisely but not too well and talk well but not too wisely."

- Somerset Maugham

Apart from convenience, many experienced cooks actually prefer to serve room temperature food and select dishes accordingly. Filet mignon is a good choice, see Recipes. As is roast chicken, lamb chops, salmon, grilled shrimp and many kinds of pasta. Also, grilled vegetables like zucchini or yellow squash, which are wonderful with just a bit of olive oil and chopped mint added after they're off the fire, or string beans with a bit of olive oil, salt and chives, see Recipes. Possibilities are endless.

Effortless, at least in the serving, are one-dish meals, such as casseroles or stews, which may only need bread or salad, or potatoes, rice or noodles on the side. Or our truly decadent noodles with prosciutto and cream all on its own. See Recipes. Stews can be a summertime thing too, one of the best we've ever had was in a bistro in Provence, a boeuf en daube with orange. Yum.

48 Spend more time with your guests than slaving in the kitchen. Food can make but seldom break an evening.

"Food is not about impressing people...it's about making them feel comfortable."

- Ina Garten

49 No tests on guests—serving a dish you haven't made before is a recipe for disaster. Believe it! Especially if unfamiliar techniques are involved.

But never complain, never explain is a good rule for any host, whether about the food or a plan that didn't work out or the condition of your home. It's so boring.

50 Plan your menu with color, flavor, texture and variety in mind. Keep it vivid, the more colorful the food, the higher the nutrients. Think beets and vitamin C, plus betaine, kale and beta-carotene (by the way, herbs and spices are also a terrific source for it, especially basil and paprika).

White on white is unappetizing. Garnish for interest but don't overdo it. You're not feeding the hamster.

51 Old Rule: Don't repeat a main ingredient, for instance, a shrimp appetizer with a shrimp main course.

New Rule
Foreshadow tastes to come—a mango chutney and cream cheese canapé preceding a mango salsa served with seared tuna main course.

52 Match the menu to the event. An elaborate roast with all the trimmings announces Holiday Dinner. Chili for the Super Bowl shouts casual, see Recipes. Oddly enough, a standing rib roast is one of the easiest dinners you can serve because potatoes and carrots can just go into the pan. A filet of beef even simpler, see Recipes.

Make interesting exceptions: Christmas in July and a picnic with your best china and crystal, or a black tie dinner in a country house deep in the woods.

Food Quantities

There's a fine balance between generous amounts and getting stuck with leftovers you have to put away at midnight. Not even chefs get this right. If you end up with too many extras, send guests home with goody bags. Have on hand a supply of inexpensive containers.

What follows are portion sizes, but make sure you have enough for seconds:

Main Course Items
Per Person

- Meat or fish: 6 - 8 oz.
- Bone-in roast: 3/4 to 1 lb.
- Boneless roast or meat in a stew: ½ lb
- Raw and leafy vegetables: 1 cup
- Other vegetables: ½ cup or 4 oz.
- Rice, grains: ½ cup or 4 oz.
- Pasta as side dish: 3 - 4 oz.; as main dish: 4 - 5 oz.; filled (ravioli): 7 oz.
- Beans (baked, lima or black beans), split peas, lentils: ½ cup
- Potatoes: 5 oz.
- Potato salad: ½ cup
- Green salad: 1 oz.

Desserts

- Mousse or pudding: 4 oz. per person
- An 8-inch round cake or tart serves 12
- A rich, dense chocolate cake serves half again as many
- A 9-inch pie serves eight
- One quart of ice cream is enough for eight

53 Head Butler's Rule: Work up a schedule of what to do and when, and a list of what's being served. Put post-its on serving pieces so you know exactly what goes where.

Ever find the rolls warming in the oven or the carrots hiding behind the cookie jar when cleaning up? We have. If you find them before morning, you can try to salvage rolls by wrapping in tin foil, re-frigerating or freezing, and adding a bit of water to each packet before warming again.

54 Our Rule: Set the table the night before. You will thank us for this. Unless priceless dinnerware is your hallmark—inherited or collected—leave the antique Spode place settings to the royals. Pottery is fine if you tend to be casual, but don't do plastic unless you know how to do it with panache.

55 Old Rule: Never seat married couples together.

New Rule
Many kinds of couples, many ways to pair them.

56 Chemistry is the key to seating people. Harry is a crashing bore, Sally loves to listen. A marriage made in heaven.

"Alternate the windbags with the hard-of-hearing."

– The New Yorker

57 If two people are hosting a dinner together, each takes one end of the table. If two tables, each presides at one. If multiple tables, some hosts may want to switch places with guests for the dessert course. This is delicate because it could interrupt a great conversation.

Some hosts like to switch everyone around for dessert, although guests may resent this. On the other hand, re-mixing changes the dynamic and sometimes strange bedfellows make good ones.

58 The host is in charge of the table.

If guests get rowdy, it's up to you to employ a diversionary tactic. Try a question: Who do you admire most in the world and why? What is your earliest memory of water? You and your guests may be amazed at what is revealed. If this doesn't bring them to heel, exit smartly to the kitchen and create a crash. Silence should be deafening. No? Then call in the SWAT team.

59 Don't impose a "discussion," political or otherwise. It's lethal and like a classroom. If a spirited debate gets started—and fisti-cuffs don't break out—you've hit the jackpot.

Get Inspired

Eight were gathered for dinner in the country on a terrace in July. As twilight settled we were asked to recall summer evenings past. Most were from childhood, one friend, an actor, reliving a moment on Cape Cod when she commanded the waves to recede, the sense of power she felt as a seven-year-old. No one was left untouched.

60 Cardinal Rule: <u>Do not shun your single friends!</u>

An inspiration from how our mothers entertained. Singles, wid-ows, widowers and divorcées were always at the table, especially, but not only, for family dinners. The most interesting of guests, it always seemed to us growing up. Because couples were more predictable? So it's sad that many singles tell us they're seldom invited, even by close friends. We're scratching our heads, wondering what these so-called friends are afraid of. An odd number? That's taking any rule too far. Or is it something else? If a single at the table is threatening, it's time for a therapist.

Music sets the mood and the host can decide what that mood should be—sultry, classic, staid, reggaeton.

"I like soundtracks from movies at dinner, especially seductive ones. A favorite is 'The View from Pompey's Head/Blue Denim,' two haunting Elmer Bernstein scores."

– Candy Pratts Price

Offer coffee with dessert, American style. But for a variation, do it European style, following dessert, which allows the addition of extra little indulgences like chocolates, bite-size cookies, macaroons, mini cupcakes or *merveilleux*, those little meringue poufs that melt in the mouth. Some refer to these as *petits fours*, from French for small ovens. Either way, it is less disruptive to serve at the table, yet another reason to have comfortable chairs.

If offering after dinner drinks, the bottles can be placed on the table.

"But where was the tour de force? The desserts were nice...the deadliest word I know about dessert."

– George Lang, in *The New Yorker*

61 End with a bang not a whimper. A killer dessert and they'll yearn to return. Your own or one prepared by a pastry chef or bakery.

Tip

A marquise, see Recipes, using the best possible chocolate can be made a day or two ahead or frozen; topped with home-whipped cream, it's a certified oohs and ahhs-getter. Or, with a few days' head start, mail-order. Sources: homebistro.com, igourmet.com, payard.com

Short Cut

Duncan Hines Dark Chocolate Fudge Brownies mix, substituting cream or half and half for the water. Dense and delicious. No one will ever guess it's from a package.

The Restaurant Dinner Party

There are times and circumstances when it is just easier and more comfortable to entertain in a restaurant. No planning, no shopping. No cooking, no cleaning up.

If you choose to gather guests in a restaurant where you're competing with ambient noise, you can achieve intimacy and cohesion with a group of say six to eight, preferably at a round table in a corner. Rules and suggestions already given about seating and hosting apply. How do we get past obsessing over the menu, which halts all talk?

Stop by and pre-select, either the entire meal or a choice between two entrees, and a reasonably priced wine or house wine. People love having the decision made for them. This also avoids the indigestion that comes with watching someone order every expensive thing on the menu or multiple courses while the rest get to sit and watch him gorge. If you choose your table, bring your own flowers, do place cards, even handwrite the menu and put a small favor at each place. It is close in feeling to entertaining at home.

Another way to do this is to suggest an evening out with the agreement that you all share the bill. You can keep the group expense in check by following some of the suggestions above. If you want to "host" part of the evening, pick up the bar tab or the tab for the wine or pay the gratuity.

No dress code needed in this era of casual when hardly any restaurants require ties and jackets—in some circles, referred to as the "Los Angelization of dining." Even the tiny minority that do require a jacket won't object if you put it over the back of the chair. About the only rule left is "don't be a slob." By the same token, we can always dress up when we feel like it or everyone decides to have a snazzy evening.

62 When organizing a dinner out, make it very clear who is paying for what.

Ted Dawson

CHAPTER SIX

Rules of Table:
Cloths and Napkins, Tableware and
Glasses, Serving

A Mad Tea Party, *Alice's Adventures in Wonderland*
Lewis Carroll

There was a table set out under a tree in front of the house, and the March Hare and the Hatter were having tea at it: a Dormouse was sitting between them, fast asleep, and the other two were using it as a cushion, resting their elbows on it, and talking over its head. 'Very uncomfortable for the Dormouse,' thought Alice; 'only, as it's asleep, I suppose it doesn't mind.'

The table was a large one, but the three were all crowded together at one corner of it: 'No room! No room!' they cried out when they saw Alice coming. 'There's plenty of room!' said Alice indignantly, and she sat down in a large arm-chair at one end of the table...

'Have some wine,' the March Hare said in an encouraging tone.

Alice looked all round the table, but there was nothing on it but tea. 'I don't see any wine,' she remarked.

'There isn't any,' said the March Hare.

'Then it wasn't very civil of you to offer it,' said Alice angrily.

'It wasn't very civil of you to sit down without being invited,' said the March Hare.

'I didn't know it was your table,' said Alice; 'it's laid for a great many more than three.'

'Your hair wants cutting,' said the Hatter. He had been looking at

Alice for some time with great curiosity, and this was his first speech.

'You should learn not to make personal remarks,' Alice said with some severity; 'it's very rude.'...

'I told you butter wouldn't suit the works!' he added looking angrily at the March Hare.

'It was the best butter,' the March Hare meekly replied.

'Yes, but some crumbs must have got in as well,' the Hatter grumbled: 'you shouldn't have put it in with the bread-knife.'

The March Hare took the watch and looked at it gloomily: then he dipped it into his cup of tea, and looked at it again: but he could think of nothing better to say than his first remark, 'It was the best butter, you know...'

This piece of rudeness was more than Alice could bear: she got up in great disgust, and walked off; the Dormouse fell asleep instantly, and neither of the others took the least notice of her going, though she looked back once or twice, half hoping that they would call after her: the last time she saw them, they were trying to put the Dormouse into the teapot.

'At any rate I'll never go there again!' said Alice as she picked her way through the wood. 'It's the stupidest tea-party I ever was at in all my life!'

Whether your table is under a tree, a tent or a golden dome, the overriding principle is comfort and a little more hospitality than telling someone they need a haircut!

63 Our Mothers' Rule: Enough elbow room to sit through several courses in comfort, six inches apart.

New Rule

Forget elbow room, rubbing elbows creates energy, and energy as we know creates heat. If you're serving, make sure you can get out without tripping over a table leg!

64 Old School Rule: 48 inches between wall and table, so guests can get in and out of chairs without banging into walls.

New Rule
36 inches suffice, a super-sized generation notwithstanding.

65 Chairs must be comfortable, whether low-backed or high.

"I believe the conversation is the essence of a party, what you eat and drink is the spice of it and a well-laid table hints of what is to come, like the wrapping on a present."

— Stanley Ager, *The Butler's Guide*

Tablecloths and Napkins

66 Traditional Rules for Tablecloths: The more formal the occasion, the longer the overhang, with measurements prescribed for each. Breakfast or lunch, 6-8 inches. Dinner, 8-12. Formal dinner, 12-18.

Lace cloths were to be placed directly on the table.

New Rule
The fundamental rules apply, if you wish, but what's wrong with a runner on a bare table and stylish place mats? Or one of the best looks we ever saw, a fine white cloth draped at the end of a large farm table, set for two.

Do we have lace cloths anymore? If we do, lace over a colored cloth is a stylish update. Check out estate sales if you like the idea.

Tips

If your cloth is too big, gather corners through napkin rings. A great look. Or tie them up with colorful ribbons.

Use pads or a felt silence cloth—or just a second cloth beneath the tablecloth. It protects the table, is more comfortable, muffles dinnerware clatter, gives a more finished look and holds the tablecloth in place.

67 Traditional Napkin Rules: The more formal the occasion, the larger the napkin. Breakfast or lunch, 12-18 inches. Dinner, 18-24. Formal dinner, 24 -32.

New Rule

Loosen up. They can be fancy paper, odd sizes, whatever suits color and tone. Men like big napkins so big works any time.

Guest Rule

Do not fold your napkin in the way it was done originally. Leave it somewhat bunched but not like a rolled up old sock in the laundry.

Houseguest Rule, speaking of laundry

Do not assume there's a laundress on staff and remove your napkin from the table. Your host may intend to seat you at the same place and use the same linen at the next meal.

Tips

A travel writer we know uses red plaid kitchen towels for napkins, whatever the occasion.

Peggy's daughter, Nicole Parker King, graphic designer and entrepreneur, sometimes uses cowboy kerchiefs in a variety of colors.

For kitchen supper contrast, use the damask napkins your mother brought out for the dowagers—again, heirloom or find at estate sales or consignment shops. Softened with age, there's nothing that feels so luxurious.

68 Fussbudget's Rule: Napkins and placemats must match.

New Rule
Mix it up. There's more of it in fashion too. How you do it may also depend on whether placemat and china are plain or patterned, the busyness of chair upholstery, the size of the table and even the room.

69 Traditional Rule: Napkins are placed on chargers or plates unless a first course is pre-set.

Even Older Rule
Never put a napkin in a wineglass.

New Rule
Put them on plates, in glasses or to the left of the fork with the fold facing the fork and plate. Are you a master of the 48 styles of napkin-folding? Go wild! No talent? Use napkins rings. No rings? Use ribbons. Tie them with costume jewelry or a rolled up horoscope, verse or limerick. Surefire way to get the fun going.

In Downton Abbey days, nothing was worse than a napkin falling out of its fold. What about a guest falling out of her bodice?

Tableware and Glasses

70 Aunt Harriet's Rule: Tableware must be of the same period—whether antique, traditional, modern, contemporary.

New Rule

If you own a range of tableware, follow Wedding Channel's two-to-one rule—one fancy to two plain elements or one plain to two fancy. Cut crystal with simple china and sleek flatware. Flowery china and ornate flatware with clean-lined stemware. You get the picture.

"Plain white china and clear glass plates are the equivalent of the little black dress. If you can afford no other, these two basics should be the foundation of your table."

– Carolyne Roehm

71 Use a charger, the table looks undressed without it. Use lacquer, rattan, smart melamine or plastic for something different.

Old Rule

If you use a charger, it must be removed before placing the dinner plate.

New Rule

Leave it as backdrop, if you like. It's an added decorative element.

72 Downton Abbey Rule: Plates are placed one inch and measured from table rim—the butler did it!—and centered on the chair.

New Rule

Forget our straitlaced forebears, lose the measuring tape. Just keep it symmetrical.

73 Logic Rule: Place flatware in order of use, from the outside working in so you don't end up eating the fish with the soup spoon.

Dessert fork and spoon are placed innermost because they are the last to be used. Alternatively, you can place them above the plate: spoon on top, bowl facing left, fork, below, tines facing right. Or, just bring them out with dessert.

Initials, monograms or patterns should be face up. Our English and Continental friends, however, do the opposite.

74 Knife blade always faces the plate.

75 Two knives and three forks are the maximum number of flatware pieces to line up for a place setting. Any more is ostentatious. Are you expecting the queen?

76 BMW Rule: **B**read plate left. **M**ain plate center. **W**ater/wine glasses right.

77 Have a set of salt and pepper for every two guests, when more than four at the table, placed along the center or between each two place settings.

78 The first glass is placed above and a little to the right of the knife. Additional glasses are arranged to its left, in order of use, from the outside in. The order when all are in play: white wine, red wine, Champagne, then the water glass or goblet farthest left so wine won't be poured into it by mistake. God forbid!

79 Use clear glass or crystal to appreciate the beauty of the wine's color. Critic Frank Prial once wrote that a $5 wine glass is fine, put the money in the wine.

Don't forget water and a lightweight pitcher to pour it from—one you can chill so you won't be flinging ice cubes all over the place when pouring.

Serving

80 **S**erve food from **l**eft, **r**emove from **r**ight. Slrr, i.e., slur, if it helps you remember.

But

81 Pour wine and water from right.

Exception
If you have an array of glasses, the water glass will be farthest left and thus less hazardous to refill from the left.

Tip
If you're serving food that's tricky to manage—oh, those rolling peas!— plating for guests is a nice gesture.

82 Richard III Rule: Host is served first, a custom from murderous days of yore when food more often than not was poisoned. If s/he keels over, hold your forks.

Ted Dawson

Commoner's Rule
The host, unless directly descended from Richard III, is last to be served.

New Rule
Serve a special guest first, if there is one, or the first woman seated to the right of the host and go around the table from there. If they all keel over, call your lawyer.

83 Traditional Rule: Guests wait for host to begin.

French Rule
The host says begin as soon as piping hot food arrives.

84 Serving dishes are passed to the right. Logic behind this rule: most people are right handed, allowing them to help themselves while their neighbor, to their left, holds the dish.

For seconds or sauces, pass dishes sideways, never across the table.

85 Vintage Rule on how to eat soup—can't you just hear Maggie Smith? Out to sea, back to me.

86 Serve no salad before wine—vinegar throws off the taste.

87 If you have several courses, keep them coming in easy rhythm. But after the main course, or salad, break for conversation to linger over the last of the dinner wine.

88 Old Rule: Clear only two plates at a time and never stack them at the table.

New Rule

It's become such a common practice that if you don't do it, a guest probably will. Just do it quietly.

Guest Rule

If your host says please don't get up from the table and clear, believe it, don't. She's trying to avoid a stampede to the kitchen.

CHAPTER SEVEN

Wine:
Pairing and Classic Couples, Decanting

State Library, South Australia: Wine in Ancient Times

According to Persian mythology, wine was discovered by a woman. She drank the fermented juice from grapes stored in a jar, went to sleep, and surprisingly woke up cured of a headache, instead of suffering from the world's first hangover as one might have expected.

Wine became the drink of the gods, whether they were Egyptian, Sumerian, or Greek, and the early deities of wine were often women, since they were also associated with fertility. The symbolism of wine, as well as its effect, became potent as it was adopted into religious ritual.

Another source of potent images, the sea, which was crucial to early transport and communication, was given the feminine gender by the Greeks. When the ancient Greek poet Homer sang of "the wine-dark sea" he was linking two forces central in Mediterranean life to create an image which continues to have great emotive power.

Julian Street in *Table Topics,* 1959, has the most often quoted passage on wine, at least in the wine industry. "Blot out every book in which wine is praised and you blot out the world's great literature, from the Bible and Shakespeare to the latest best-seller. Blot out the wine-drinkers of the world and you blot out history, including saints, philosophers, statesmen, soldiers, scientists, and artists."

Wines today have undergone a sea change. The once-snooty wine industry has loosened up: White Trash White, Woodcutters Red, and Fat Bastard Chardonnay have all been popular labels. Then there's Scraping the Barrel, a Tempranillo from Spain, whose back label suggests it be drunk with chips and gravy. But the prize for irreverence has to go to Cat's Pee on a Gooseberry Bush, a Sauvignon Blanc from New Zealand.

Some people still pursue wines like The Holy Grail, adhering strictly to the catechism of Robert Parker or some other wine guru. If that's your approach, fine, just don't expect everyone to share this level of interest. Drinking wine is above all a pleasurable experience, best enjoyed when we're relaxed about it. Some principles do apply which enhance the experience and reassure the host.

You may want to begin a dinner party gathering with an aperitif, a before-dinner type wine. Dubonnet and Lillet come to mind, or dry sherry or a specialty drink like Campari, or a simple white or light red wine. This wine will not be your best because you want the focus to be on mingling and talking.

Nothing promotes mingling like bubbly. The business of peeling the foil, unscrewing the wire, thumbing off the cork, and listening for the pop and fizz puts everyone in the mood to party. It goes great with anything salty from Beluga caviar to peanuts. Timing is everything. For more fun assemble everyone for the ritual.

"I drink Champagne when I'm happy and when I'm sad. Sometimes I drink it when I'm alone. When I have company, I consider it obligatory. I trifle with it if I'm not hungry, and drink it when I am. Otherwise I never touch it-unless I'm thirsty."

- Madame Bollinger

If you are having cocktails and distilled spirits are flowing freely, palates may be numb by the time food is on the table. Don't bother with the fine wines.

Not even diehard enthusiasts agree on rules for pairing wines with food. But there is one fundamental all agree on:

89 More than one course, launch with the least of the wines and progress to the best. The royal exception is Sauternes with foie gras and the noblest of all Sauternes is from Château d'Yquem. An okay cheat is an American version, sauterne, no capital "s" and no "s" on the end. Whichever you serve, chill for no more than an hour and a half.

90 Allow half a bottle of wine per person through dinner, but with four or five courses over a period of several hours, up to a bottle per person.

Tip
No co-host? Ask a guest to help pour. A bottle at either end of the table keeps the wine flowing.

"If more of us valued food and cheer and song above hoarded gold, it would be a merrier world."

— J.R.R. Tolkien

91 Fill the wine glass to its widest point—about half—so you can swirl and savor the bouquet.

Tip
Using the appropriate glass for the type of wine increases your pleasure the way tea in a porcelain cup tastes better than in a mug.

Pairing

92 Traditional Rules for pairing: Red wine with red meat; white wine with white meat, fish or poultry. Sweet wine with sweet food, acidic with acidic, spicy with spicy.

Some of this is simply matching of flavors. The citrus quality of sauvignon blanc works well with fish in the same way lemon does.

Wine lecturer and French-trained chef Stephen Reiss' Rule
White with light, red with rich.

Writer and wine buff David Duffy's Rule
Don't be afraid to experiment. For example, Riesling, a German classic, is a terrific match with many Asian cuisines.

If you live in a wine producing region you will likely know those wines well and will serve them confidently with most dishes. It can also be fun to choose wines from the same country as the food, Rioja with paella, for example.

93 Match wine to sauce for fish, likewise with pasta.

94 Dry before sweet, young before old, white before red.

Classic Couples

Over the years, some pairings have taken hold,
which are useful to know about:
- Salmon and pinot noir
- Lobster and Chardonnay
- Gumbos and other spicy foods and Zinfandel
- Oysters and Chablis but also Champagne
- Grilled chicken and Beaujolais
- Lamb and red Bordeaux
- Beef with red Burgundy or cabernet sauvignon
- Braised beef with Barolo
- Chocolate and cabernet sauvignon
- Stilton cheese with walnuts and Port

Duffy's Tips on Decanting

Decant very young reds to give a head start on opening up, but this can also be done in the glass.

Decant very old reds to settle sediment if you enjoy the ritual, but standing the bottle upright for a day will also settle the sediment—just pour carefully.

For all other reds, pour from the bottle as you go through the evening to taste the changing nature of the wine as it mixes with air. This makes for a fuller experience.

"Quickly, bring me a beaker of wine, so I may wet my mind and say something clever."

- Aristophanes

95 Champagne may be served with dessert or after. A bottle fills 8-10 flutes. But many people prefer a sweet wine—Sauternes would top any such list—or a sweet sparkling wine, such as Asti; a crémant from France (meaning sparkling wine not from Champagne); a lovely lemony vin santo from Italy; or, for a change and a beautiful looking wine, a sparkling rosé.

96 Never pair a wine with food that is sweeter than it is. Dessert wines, therefore, are only offered after dessert. A bottle of dessert wine is sufficient for ten.

97 Dessert Wine Rule: Chill but remove from refrigerator about 20 minutes before serving. Pour small, meaning 2-3 ounces, about half the usual pour. If you don't believe us on the chill, compare a dessert wine or Champagne with greater or lesser chilling time and decide which delivers more flavor.

CHAPTER EIGHT

Specialty Parties:
Dessert Party, Open House or Big Bash

The Dessert Party

A sweet and simple way to entertain. Dessert parties are usually on the late side, say after nine and after dinner, but suit yourself and your guests. To the true sweet tooth, this will be dinner. For 12 or more guests, offer at least seven selections—even more if you want to make it sumptuous. Most desserts freeze really well so leftovers will not be wasted. In honor of evening shadows, have lots of candles of all shapes and sizes. Consider Champagne or sparkling wines, light liqueurs such as Limoncello or Amaretto, and have fun with flavored coffees.

To the obvious cakes and pies, add mini tarts and mini cheesecakes. For those who are just dropping by, include easy pick-ups in the mix—brownies, cookies, lemon bars. Or goat cheese on toast points—Petits Toasts of Trois Petits Cochons are great topped with jellies from mint to jalapeno. Fruits and cheeses provide varying tastes and textures—Bel Paese and pears, cheddar and apples, goat cheese and mangos, brie and strawberries are all sublime partners. Dishes of glazed nuts and candies should abound.

Everyone goes home with sugarplums dancing in their heads.

Open House/The Big Bash

If it's holiday time or a milestone event, the way to go is the big bash. Granddad is turning 80 and you have to have the relatives, even if they behave like The Sopranos, along with Granny's knitting circle and folks from church or temple. If it's a really big bash, stagger times on the invitations. You'll be glad they didn't all come at once. This is one time you may want staid.

Get Inspired

The family gathered for the celebration of a lifetime, the 90th birthday of their patriarch. Accolades from yearbooks, articles and letters were inserted into fortune cookies, the originals having been tweezered out. Without prompting, children, grandchildren and great-grandchildren jumped up to read the tributes to their beloved "PopPop."

Another favorite was an Argentine barbecue in Miami, featuring, what else? Marinated steaks (if not from Argentina, who's to know?) and a chimichurri sauce of chopped garlic and parsley, along with empanadas, pitchers of Sangria and BA Bellinis made with Freixenet, napkins tied with mini riatas, Latin music and tangos on the terrace. Our host was decked out in gaucho pants, hat and apron. Was that olé we heard him shouting?

Managing the flow of a crowd works best when you line up dishes along both sides of the table. Arrange them in order of the meal: easy to sample appetizers for those who may not want more, main course(s), sides, salad, desserts. Plates should be stacked at the beginning, with forks and spoons wrapped in napkins at the end. Have plenty of extras for those who decide on seconds but have already turned in their plates and utensils.

Tips

Stations are more fun than one long table, if you have room. Or set up a second table for desserts.

Forcing guests to juggle plates while clutching a glass of wine or juice is cruel and unusual punishment. Scatter little tables around—rent or borrow. This way, you won't find overturned glasses on the carpet in the morning, a truly depressing sight.

98 Bite-size pieces are the rule and food that doesn't require a knife. It's clumsy cutting meat on your lap and impossible when standing. Small bites won't impede conversation either. Avoid food that's difficult to manage, like buttered noodles or corn on the cob.

99 When serving buffet style, increase quantities by one-third over a dinner party—people eat more than at a sit-down dinner. But, the more choices on offer, the more grazing, and each portion size taken will be smaller.

100 Less for the older crowd, more for the younger. Less in hot weather, more in cold.

101 Nanny Rule: If you want adults to have a good time, keep children occupied. Get someone to organize activities for them or put out the word, caregivers welcome.

Tips

Small fries delight in anything pint-sized—mini burgers, pancakes, cupcakes kids can decorate, mini chocolate chip cookies. What fun to brag you've had four burgers, six pancakes and a dozen cookies!

Multiplying recipes as we have noted is tricky. Ingredients and cooking times are not increased in the way you might think is logical. Generally speaking, use only recipes geared to a crowd. Consult Susan Wyler's Cooking for a Crowd, *Ina Garten's* Barefoot Contessa Parties, Moosewood Restaurant Cooks for a Crowd.

Target and some supermarkets have "designer" melamine, plastic or paper plates and cups. For a more upscale look, rent from a local caterer, scoop up sale items at a party warehouse, or collect from garage or estate sales.

Bright lacquer or patterned trays are another way to add color, and they are efficient transport too. But trays can be treacherous. Even more efficient is using a cardboard box with sides for stability. If you want to leave it on the bar, line it with tin foil or attractive shelf paper. Otherwise, place a towel on the bottom and turn over the glasses—typically can fit more of them this way. Whether tray or box, add a long-stemmed rose or peony.

For barbecues and picnics, colorful plastic tubs from Home Depot or a child's wagon can be filled with ice to chill wine, beer and soft drinks. So can your top-loading clothes washer, believe it or not! Just a spin cycle afterwards to get rid of melted ice.

Less colorful but practical and economical for outdoors are large trash cans, appropriately marked to distinguish recyclables from trash.

If you entertain a lot, keep track if you want to avoid serving the same dishes to the same guests. Likewise with décor, flowers, theme, guest lists, linens, wines and table drama. Take pictures of your table setting. Start scrapbooking. Make notes in your iPhone Yellow Pad. Keep a party journal.

The Last Word Belongs to Jane Austen and Her Modern Muse
A Modern Take on a Jane Austen Soireé

It's funny how you never hear "role-playing" and "Jane Austen" in the same sentence, especially when you consider all that fanfic out there. So, if you are really feeling adventurous, I suggest designing some sort of Austen role-playing activity. You could, you know, assign the different parts from a book beforehand, get everyone together, and let them have at it. Sounds sort of like Lost in Austen, doesn't it?

Or, why not do a Pride and Prejudice and Zombies flash mob? Everyone decide beforehand whether you'll be a zombie, a Bennet sister, or an innocent bystander; show up someplace and have it out! Regency zombie battles on the National Mall! I see this happening, people! Serious Austen party-ers will do this in full costume, of course. But watch where you put that sword. You could put someone's eye out with that thing.

Whenever you get together, you are probably having a party pretty close to one Jane Austen wrote! Oh, the food, drink, dancing, and clothes might be different, but I bet the social dynamics are not far off. I know that's not what you want to hear, though, so I suggest the Jane Austen Olympics! Events can include: the 100-meter Dash Across the Lawn to Find Mr. Bennet, the All-Terrain Walk to Netherfield (points deducted per inch of dirty hem), the Louisa Musgrove Stair-Jumping Contest, the Pairs' Rainy Hillside Rescue Dance, Fencing Wits, and Conversational Gymnastics (Lizzie's an odds-on favorite there, clearly), and...

...But you see! The possibilities are endless! Now get your corsets on, go out there, and PARTY!!!

Austenacious Web Site

RECIPES

A Dozen Favorites

"The most remarkable thing about my mother is that for 30 years she served the family nothing but leftovers. The original meal has never been found."

- Calvin Trillin

So many recipes, so little time, how to choose? The dozen here, from appetizers to desserts, have been favorites over the years, tasty and relatively fuss-free. More great ideas are at our fingertips, of course, on the Web.

- Mom's Crabmeat Canapé
- The Mystery Canapé Everyone Loves
- Endive Salad
- Greenbean Salad
- Shrimp Scampi
- Baked Potatoes with Mushrooms and/or Chili Stuffing
- Chicken Cacciatore with Potatoes
- Bouillabaisse
- Nouilles a la Crème or Truly Decadent Noodles
- Roast Filet of Beef
- Plum Crisp
- Chocolate Marquise

Plus For Fun· Chicken Hash from the Plaza Hotel and Ina Garten's Version

Terms of Ingredients:

- Butter means unsalted
- Olive oil means extra virgin
- Salt means kosher or sea salt
- Packaged broth means Kitchen Basics brand, so superior

Equipment:

Equipment beyond the obvious measuring tools, scrapers, etc.
Pasta pot, colander, saucepan(s), large Dutch oven (often called a casserole), cheese grater, large nonstick skillet(s) or sauté pan(s), with cover and utensils that can be used with nonstick, baking sheet, cooling rack, 8x4 glass baking pan or loaf pan, 8x8 baking pan, shallow roasting pan, double boiler, whisk.

Mom's Crabmeat Canapé
8 to 10 Servings

1 package (8 ounces) Philadelphia cream cheese at room temperature
6 - 8 ounces fresh, frozen or canned lump crabmeat, well picked over
1 bottle Crosse & Blackwell seafood sauce
1/2 lemon
½ teaspoon horseradish
Triskets and spreading knife

Mash crabmeat into cream cheese with a fork and mound mixture on a dinner plate. Add lemon juice and horseradish to seafood sauce, to taste, and spread over mixture. Surround with Triskets, spreading knife. Can be done by host.

Mystery Dip
8 to 10 Servings

1 can artichoke hearts in water, drained and chopped
1 cup mayonnaise
1 teaspoon diced onion
1 cup freshly-grated Parmigiano-Reggiano cheese
¼ teaspoon cayenne
Carr's water biscuits for serving

Preheat oven to 350°. Mix all ingredients in ceramic bowl and pour into 8-inch glass baking dish. Bake about 30 minutes or until it starts to bubble. Remove from oven and serve while warm on Carr's water biscuits.

Green Beans as Salad
6 Servings

1 pound green beans, stem end snipped off - slim French beans are best
Lemon flavored olive oil, about a tablespoon
Sea salt
Chives, optional

In a saucepan, bring to a boil enough water to cover beans. Add beans, bring back to boil for 2-2 ½ minutes. Drain in colander. Turn out into bowl, drizzle with lemon flavored olive oil (using fresh lemon discolors warm beans), add snipped chives, if using, and toss. Sprinkle with sea salt. Serve room temperature.

Belgian Endive with Blue Cheese and Roasted Pecans
6 Servings

6 Belgian endive
3 tablespoons olive oil
1 tablespoon lemon juice
Salt and pepper
¾ cup blue or Roquefort cheese, crumbled
¾ cup pecan halves, roasted
1 ½ tablespoons brown sugar
1 ½ tablespoons butter

In large nonstick skillet, melt butter and stir in brown sugar and pecan halves. Cook 5 minutes medium heat, stirring often, being careful not to scorch the nuts. Turn out onto plate, separating any clumps that formed, and sprinkle lightly with sea salt. Mix olive oil and lemon juice, season with salt and pepper. Trim ends and rinse whole endives. Pat dry and cut crosswise, then in strips lengthwise. Toss with oil and lemon juice mixture, cheese and nuts.

Shrimp Scampi
4 Servings

Easy to double but use two large skillets or cook in two batches.
Good with pasta too, linguini fini or something equally slim, with olive oil, a chopped up fresh tomato, black olives if on hand. Pasta here is a side dish so about half a pound for four.

3 tablespoons butter
2 tablespoons olive oil
4 garlic cloves, minced
1/2 cup dry white wine or broth
3/4 teaspoon salt, or to taste
1/8 teaspoon red pepper flakes, or to taste
Freshly ground black pepper
1 3/4 pounds large or extra-large shrimp
1/3 cup chopped parsley or chives, juice of half a lemon + 1 teaspoon grated rind (zest)

Shell shrimp - easier by cutting along tops with scissors and pulling apart shells. Pull out veins. In large skillet, melt butter with olive oil, low heat. Add garlic and sauté about 1 minute, careful not to brown. Add wine or broth, salt, red pepper flakes and plenty of black pepper and bring to simmer, about 2 minutes. Add shrimp and sauté until just pink, 2 to 3 minutes depending on size. Stir in parsley or chives, lemon juice and zest.

Baked Potatoes Stuffed with Mushrooms and/or Chili
6-8 Servings

Potatoes
In 450° oven, 6 or 8 baking potatoes, lightly greased with olive oil, pierced 3 or 4 times each with a fork to release steam and placed di-

rectly on oven rack. Bake 45 minutes, check with fork or knife to see if tender. Remove with tongs or oven mitts. Place on serving platter. Cut each lengthwise and gently spread open. Scoop out some of potato or use it all.

Mushrooms

3 pounds mushrooms, rinsed, patted dry and sliced (mix of button, shitake, cremini, Portobello)

3 tablespoons of butter + 3 tablespoons olive oil

3 minced garlic cloves

3-4 minced shallots

1 cup white or red wine

2 tablespoons dried thyme (or more to taste), plus salt and fresh ground pepper

In large sauté pan (or two of them or in two batches to accommodate mushrooms), heat butter and olive oil medium-high. Add garlic, shallots and sauté a few minutes. Add mushrooms and reduce to medium. Cook 10-15 minutes or until starting to brown. Add wine, thyme and stir. Salt and pepper to taste. Can also add 3 tablespoons cream at end.

Chili

To serve as chili alone double this recipe for 10-12

1 tablespoon olive oil

1/2 pound ground pork

1/2 pound ground beef

1/2 pound chuck steak, fat trimmed, cut into 1-inch cubes; butcher should do this for you

3 garlic cloves, minced

1 cup water

1 tablespoon ground cumin

1 tablespoon chili powder

1 teaspoon dried oregano

1 teaspoon salt

½ teaspoon cayenne pepper

1 to 1 ½ 6-ounce cans tomato paste

1 teaspoon sugar

1 ½ cups diced fresh tomatoes

1 ½ cups diced onions

1 ½ cups diced red bell peppers

1 ½ cups canned black beans, drained, rinsed (two 15-ounce cans; use both if you like)

½ cup chopped fresh cilantro + additional for topping if you like

1 ¼ cups beef broth

1 cup or 4 ounces grated cheddar cheese, for topping

Lime slices, sour cream, optional

Heat olive oil in large pot over medium-high heat. Add ground pork and ground beef, sauté until brown, about 3 minutes. Add cubed beef and garlic, sauté 5 minutes. Add water, bring to boil. Add seasonings. Reduce heat, cover, simmer 10 minutes. Add tomato paste and sugar, simmer 5 minutes. Add tomatoes, onions, peppers, simmer until vegetables are tender, about 30 minutes. Add black beans and cilantro. Add beef broth, ¼ cup at a time, until thinned to desired consistency. (Can be prepared 1 day ahead. Refrigerate uncovered until cold, then cover.) Before serving, bring chili to simmer. Spoon onto potatoes. Top with grated cheddar and serve.

Chicken Cacciatore with Potatoes
6 Servings

This is usually served with pasta but for an all in one dish, use potatoes instead.

¼ pound pancetta or regular bacon sliced crosswise

4 pound frying chicken, in pieces with each breast half cut in two, salted and peppered

2 tablespoons olive oil, one tablespoon butter – less if bacon fat

1 medium onion, chopped, about a cup

1 green pepper, chopped

bay leaf

1 teaspoon dried rosemary or thyme

1 teaspoon dried sage

2 cloves garlic, chopped

½ cup white or red wine

14-ounce can of plum tomatoes with their juices

¾ cup chicken broth

¾ pound mushrooms, in halves or thirds – browned separately for better flavor, or not

4 small to medium white potatoes, about a pound, cut in quarters

Chopped parsley, optional

In large skillet, sauté pancetta or bacon in small bit of olive oil. If using bacon, oil not needed. Drain on paper towel on plate. Brown chicken in bacon fat, if any, plus/minus 2 tablespoons olive oil and 1 tablespoon butter (butter helps in browning) over medium high heat. Do in batches, remove to plate. Pour off fat, except 2 tablespoons. On medium heat, sauté onions and green pepper with bay leaf and dried herbs about 5 minutes. Add garlic for a minute more. Add back chicken. Add wine, tomatoes and their juice, broth. Cover and cook, low heat, 20 minutes. Meanwhile, cut potatoes in quarters, cover with water, bring to boil, simmer about 10 minutes, until just tender, drain and set aside. Sauté mushrooms medium high heat until lightly browned. Add mushrooms, potatoes and bacon to chicken and cook 10 minutes more. Serve with chopped parsley.

Bouillabaisse á la David Duffy
8 Servings

Cutting vegetables takes the time here but most of this can be cooked a day ahead. Final cooking takes just minutes, the most forgiving of fish dishes. Terrific next day too. Especially good with corn bread. Note: some recipes specify croutons, this one does not.

2 tablespoons olive oil + 2 tablespoons butter

2 medium leeks

4 largish shallots

2 small to medium fennel bulbs

2 medium celery stalks

2 bay leaf

½ teaspoon fennel seeds, ground

½ teaspoon saffron threads, not essential

6 cloves garlic, minced

2 tablespoons tomato paste, dissolved in 2 tablespoons water

1 cup white wine

2 28-ounce cans San Marzano tomatoes, roughly chopped

5-6 cups fish or seafood stock*

1 teaspoon salt

1 teaspoon black pepper

2 shakes red pepper flakes

2 pounds fish (cod, monk, sea bass, halibut, hake)

1 ½ pounds shrimp

1 pound lump crab meat - if difficult to find, leave out, but it adds wonderful flavor

4 tablespoons Ouzo - worth buying for this, not as strong as Pernod and less expensive

Juice from 1 Meyer lemon, if available

Trim tough green parts off leek, halve lengthwise, wash carefully in basin or bowl, cut into half-inch lengths. Remove tops and quarter fennel bulbs, core, slice thinly. Quarter shallots lengthwise, slice. Halve celery lengthwise, slice crosswise. Heat oil and butter in large casserole pot over medium low, add vegetables, bay leaf, saffron and ground fennel bulbs, and sauté without browning until tender, about 10 minutes, stirring from time to time. Add garlic, cook two minutes more. Add tomato paste, stir one minute. Stir in wine, bring to boil and boil gently three minutes. Add tomatoes, fish stock, red pepper flakes, salt and pepper. Blend thoroughly, bring to boil, cover, simmer 20 minutes. Can do this far up to day in advance, refrigerate and reheat.

Cut fish into 1 ½ inch pieces. Halve shrimp if large. Add fish to simmering broth, simmer two minutes. Add shrimp, simmer two minutes. Add crab meat, ouzo, simmer one minute. Remove from heat and stir in Meyer lemon juice, if using.

*He makes his own stock, using *Joy of Cooking* recipe, but including shrimp shells.

Nouilles a la Crème or
Truly Decadent Noodles
4-6 Servings

½ pound mushrooms, sliced thin
1 small zucchini, not peeled, sliced thin
4 tablespoons butter
2 cloves garlic, crushed
1/3 cup parsley, minced
¼ pound prosciutto, cut in thin strips, or julienne
1 cup heavy cream
1/3 cup Parmesan
Salt and pepper to taste
1 pound fettuccini

In a bowl, mix parsley with prosciutto and garlic. Sauté mushrooms and zucchini in butter over high heat, shaking pan, till liquid evaporates. Add garlic, prosciutto and parsley mixture and sauté 2 - 3 minutes. Add cream and cook 2-3 minutes. Remove garlic—if bits of it are left behind, no problem. Toss with cooked fettuccini, salt and fresh ground pepper. Add Parmesan. Toss again.

Filet of Beef, 4-5 pounds trimmed
8-10 servings

Give us 22 minutes, we'll give you the world, or so goes the slogan of a local radio station. In 22 to 25 minutes, you can give guests a perfect filet of beef. It can be served warm or it can hang around all day. Serve with horseradish sauce or mushroom mélange, see recipe for Baked Potatoes Stuffed with Mushrooms. Have it trimmed well—supermarket butchers will do this. You may have leftovers. Steak BLT's for lunch? Potatoes au gratin are wonderful with this.

1 filet, trimmed and at room temperature, meaning out of the fridge one hour
2 tablespoons butter and oil
Salt and fresh ground pepper

Preheat oven to 425°. Brown filet quickly on top of stove in large skillet in butter and olive oil, about a tablespoon total, about a minute a side, sprinkling with grainy salt and freshly ground pepper, up to 1 tablespoon of each. Transfer to shallow roasting pan. Or skip the browning and rub with 2 tablespoons oil and melted butter, salt and pepper. Roast 22 to 25 minutes for rare. Remove, cover loosely with tin foil and rest 15-20 minutes before slicing. Serve with mushroom mélange, if using.

Another simple partner: roasted tomatoes with garlic and Parmesan. In 400° oven, in 8x8 baking dish, 2 boxes or pints cherry tomatoes spread on top of ¼ cup (2 ounces) grated Parmesan, drizzled with 2 ta-

blespoons olive oil, 2 chopped garlic cloves, salt and pepper. Shake dish to coat. Bake 15 minutes, until tomatoes start to split. Scrape into bowl and serve on the side.

The Plaza Hotel Chicken Hash
4-5 Servings

"Chicken Hash for Capote's party? Well if you've ever tasted the food that came out of the Plaza Hotel's catering department, you might have found that a wise choice. Truman, it seemed, had known the limitations of the Plaza kitchens. He chose something so home-spun and forgiving, they couldn't really screw it up. There must have been an excess of cream at the Plaza's kitchen on the day they invented this sauce. Can you imagine, heavy cream AND cream sauce AND Hollandaise for that small amount of chicken? Makes my arteries clog just thinking about it. Needless to say I have never tried this recipe so proceed at your own risk!

"Since Ina Garten would have been about 18 when the Ball took place, Truman couldn't have had the supreme good fortune of serving her Chicken Hash. But I have on numerous occasions, most recently on a cold night when I had half a roast chicken left over and a yearning for some real comfort food. This dish, with its crispy potatoes and onions, its lovely chunks of red pepper and breast of chicken all laced together with a very flavorful spice mix, is absolutely delicious. Ina's recipe calls for roasting bone-in chicken breasts rather than using leftovers. I've done it both ways and believe me when I say, it's worth the effort to roast the breasts. It just takes a little longer. Even with the roasting, the dinner takes just over an hour to make and the prep time is about 45 minutes all told. So raise a glass to both Ina and Truman and make this delicious dish."

- Monte Mathews
writing in his food blog www.chewingthefat.us.com
on the 45th Anniversary of Truman Capote's Black and White Ball

Continued on next page...

4 cups finely diced cooked chicken (white meat only)

1 1/2 cup heavy cream

1 cup cream sauce (béchamel)

2 teaspoons salt

1/8 teaspoon white pepper

1/4 cup dry Sherry

1/2 cup Hollandaise Sauce

Mix chicken, cream, cream sauce, salt and pepper in heavy, ovenproof skillet. Cook moderate heat, stirring often, about 10 minutes. When moisture is slightly reduced, place skillet in 350° oven and bake 30 minutes. Stir in Sherry and return to oven 10 minutes. Lightly fold in Hollandaise Sauce. Serve at once.

Ina Garten's Basil Chicken Hash
4 Servings

2 whole (4 split) chicken breasts, bone-in, skin-on

16 basil leaves

Olive Oil

Kosher salt and freshly ground black pepper

6 tablespoons , divided

2 pounds boiling potatoes, preferably Yukon Golds, peeled and large diced

2 red peppers, chopped

2 onions, large, diced

3 garlic cloves, minced

2 teaspoons fresh thyme leaves

1 teaspoon paprika

1 tablespoon tomato paste

4 minced scallions, white and green parts

Sour cream, and sliced lemons, for serving

Heat oven to 350°. Place chicken on sheet pan. Loosen skin, leaving one side attached. Place 4 basil leaves under skin of each breast. Pull skin over as much of meat as possible so chicken won't dry out. Rub each piece with olive oil and sprinkle generously with salt and pepper. Bake chicken for 35 to 40 minutes, until skin is lightly browned and chicken is just cooked through. Set aside until cool enough to handle, then remove meat from bones. Cut chicken in large dice pieces and set aside. Melt 4 tablespoons of the butter in a large sauté pan. Add the potatoes and onions, 1 teaspoon salt and 1/2 teaspoon pepper and sauté over medium heat for about 10 minutes, until evenly browned and cooked through. In a separate sauté pan, melt the remaining 2 tablespoons of butter. Add the red peppers, garlic, thyme, paprika, tomato paste, 1 teaspoon salt and 1/2 teaspoon pepper and sauté over medium heat for about 5 minutes, until the edges of the peppers are seared. Add the chicken and the pepper mixture to the potatoes and heat through. Add the scallions and parsley, toss together and place on a serving platter.

Plum Crisp
8 Servings

Filling
4 cups sliced plums - 2 to 2 ½ pounds
1 tablespoon all-purpose flour
2 tablespoons sugar
1 teaspoon vanilla
1/2 teaspoon cinnamon

Topping
1/2 cup all-purpose flour
1/2 cup oats
1/2 cup brown sugar
1/8 teaspoon salt
1/4 cup butter, melted

Preheat oven to 350°. In a medium-size bowl toss plums, flour, sugar, vanilla, and cinnamon together. Pour into un-greased 1 1/2-quart baking dish. In a small bowl combine topping ingredients and mix with fork until crumbly. Spread topping mixture evenly over plums (use hands for this). Bake 40 to 45 minutes or until topping is crispy and golden brown. Serve with vanilla ice cream or freshly whipped cream.

Chocolate Marquise (Grande Marquise au Chocolat)
6-10 Servings

This is the killer dessert, the one that ends the dinner with a bang not a whimper! Yes, it takes time but...

What's great about this recipe is that it goes in the freezer, so you can make a day ahead and leftovers (seldom any) can be put back in the freezer for up to a month. Serve with heavy cream whipped with a little powdered sugar. Alternatively, serve a slice with a ball of ice cream and a few raspberries and MWAH!

6 ounces Hershey's Milk Chocolate
6 ounces Lindt Bittersweet Chocolate
4 ounces Ghirardelli Semi-sweet Chocolate
1/2 stick unsalted butter
6 large eggs separated, plus yolks of two more eggs
Pinch of salt
1/2 pint heavy cream or ice cream

Butter a loaf pan or 8x4 glass baking dish. Line it with long sheet of plastic wrap lengthwise to overhang about five inches on each side. Then line with plastic wrap crosswise to also overhang about five inches. Melt chocolate and butter in top of a double boiler, not over direct heat, stirring with wooden spoon. Off heat, whisk in sugar until completely blended. Beat in all eight egg yolks, one at a time, until incorporated. You don't want eggs to curdle, but you do want the hot mixture to gently cook them. Add pinch of salt.

Beat the six eggs whites in a deep bowl with a wire whisk until they form soft peaks. (A large, cold copper bowl will expedite the beating). Fold one-third of egg whites into chocolate/butter/eggs mixture. Then fold in the second and then the third until well incorporated. Transfer to loaf pan or glass dish, make sure it's spread into all corners and smooth out the top. Cover with overhanging plastic wrap. Bundle it up in aluminum foil and freeze for at least five hours. To serve, unwrap the foil and the plastic. Run a knife dipped in warm water around the edge of the pan to loosen. Put a serving plate on top of the marquise and invert it onto the plate. Slice with sharp knife, not too thick as this is a rich dessert.

About the Authors

Peggy Healy is Executive Vice President, Montgomery Communications, in Manhattan, specialist in travel, particularly unique properties in Africa and Europe. Co-author of the highly successful *Salute to Italy Celebrity Cookbook*, she has been a contributing editor of *Dallas Home and Garden* and is a former operating vice president of Bloomingdale's.

Marcelline Thomson, a writer who lives in the Hudson Valley, has recently finished a novel, *Dreaming of Oranges*. Formerly a Managing Director of Ogilvy Adams & Rinehart, a leading New York corporate and financial public relations firm, she has ghost written a memoir, among other free lance projects.

About the Designer

Vicky Forsyth-Smith is a student at New York's School of Visual Arts and recipient of its second-largest scholarship. She designed a sweatshirt for Miley Cyrus that was sold on her tour and has won various fine arts awards. This is her first book to free lance design. See more of her work at www.vicky.nyc.

16300635R00073

Made in the USA
Middletown, DE
11 December 2014